A QUANTUM BOOK

Published by
Chartwell Books
A Division of Book Sales, Inc.
114 Northfield Avenue
Edison, New Jersey, 08837
USA

ISBN 0-7858-0676-8

This book was produced by
Quantum Books Ltd
6 Blundell Street
London N7 9BH

Produced in Australia by Griffin Colour

Jewelry
MAKING

JINKS McGRATH

CHARTWELL
BOOKS, INC.

Essential Tools

Your first requirement is a table or bench on which to work. The kitchen table may do to start with, but I would not recommend it for the long term. The sooner you can find a little corner of your own where you can safely leave your work unattended, the better! An old table will make a suitable bench, but make sure that it has sturdy legs. The recommended height for all benches is about 36 inches, which will give support to your elbows while you are sitting in an upright position.

You can make your own workbench by using a sheet of 1 inch plywood, 48 × 72 inches. Cut a semicircle approximately 24 inch across in the center of one of the long sides. Anchor the table top to a firm base, making sure that nothing obstructs the semicircular opening. Fasten a strong piece of muslin or leather around the underside of the semicircle, holding it in place with hooks. This will catch all the filings and scrap metal pieces, which can be taken to a refiner and sold.

A useful and portable workbench. It should be anchored to the floor to give maximum stability.

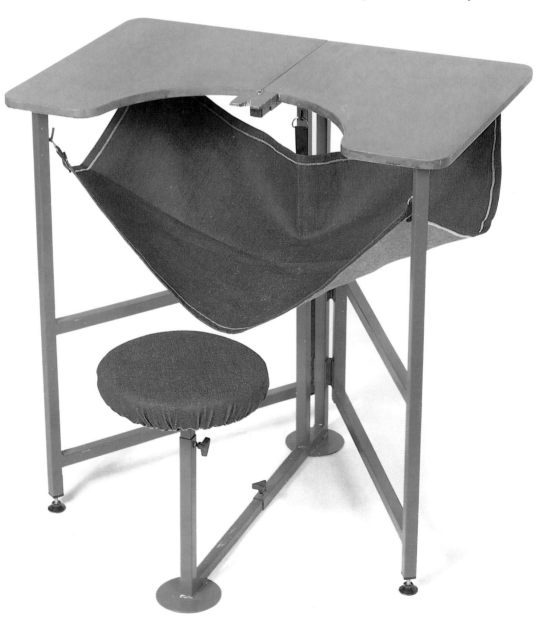

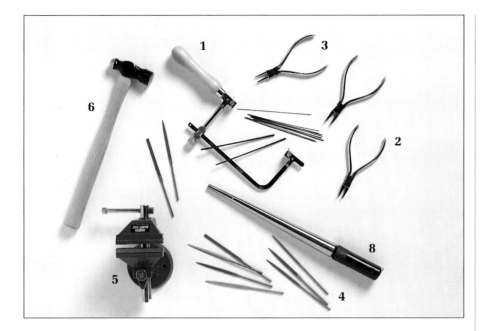

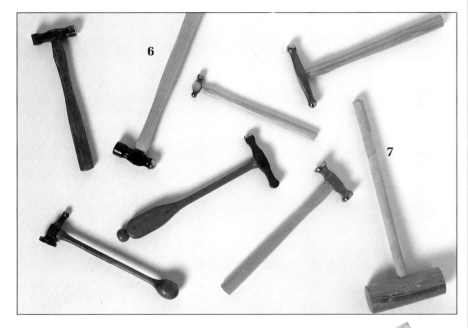

1 Jeweler's saw and blades You will keep this tool forever. The blades come in packs of 12, and it is cheaper to buy a gross. Start off with blade numbers 2/0, 1/0 and 1.

2 Flat-nose pliers Buy two pairs of pliers, with oval ends or with straight ends. Keep a look out for a very small pair.

3 Round-nose pliers These are useful for bending wire, and you should get a large pair and a small pair.

4 Needle files These are used extensively for refining shapes, removing solder, and leveling surfaces, and you will need flat, oval, triangular, and semicircular ones. Needle files are available in packets of 8 or 10, and this is a good way to buy them.

5 Small vise There are two different sorts of vise that you will find useful. A jeweler's vise has a ball joint, which means that it can be used in all angles, and "safe" jaws. A small bench vise (see opposite) is sturdier for most jobs, and you can make your own safe jaws from copper or wood if necessary.

6 Hammer A general-purpose hammer is called a ball-peen (or ball-pein) hammer.

7 Mallet Wooden and rawhide mallets are generally used to shape silver because they do not leave marks.

8 Mandrel This tool is a steel rod essential for shaping rings, wires, collets, and so on after soldering. It is also sometimes known as a triblet.

BENCH PIN

Whether you are working on the kitchen table or have made your own bench, you will need what is called a "pin." This is a wedge of wood fitted to the center of the semicircle in the bench or held on a table with a C-clamp. Some jewelers cut a V in the middle of the wedge so that the silver can rest on the wood while the piercing saw works up the V. It also supports the work while it is being filed, cleaned, set, burnished, and so on. In other words, it is a vital part of your equipment.

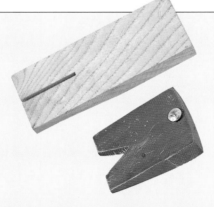

A pin that is suitable to fix to a transportable workbench (below) and an example of a permanent fixture on a bench (above).

Recommended Tools

Listed here are some of the other useful tools that are worth watching out for as you progress with your skills.

KEY:

1 Riffler files
2 Wooden punches
3 Ring sizers
4 Doming block
5 Anvil or flatplate
6 Arkansas stone
7 Large files

8 Drawplates
9 Top cutters/side cutters
10a Half-round pliers
10b Parallel pliers
10c Serrated pliers
11 Crucible
12 Scriber or scribe
13a Drill bits
13b Bow drill

13c Hand vise or drill
14 Metal punches
15 Swage block
16 Burnishers
17 Suede stick and emery sticks
18 Sandbag
19 Hand vise and ring clamp
20 Jointing tool

1 Riffler files These curved files allow you to file in corners, on curves, and in generally inaccessible places.

2 Wooden punches Punches are used for all sorts of "forming" work. Wooden ones shape without marking, and it is useful to have a range of diameters.

3 Ring sizers These come in sizes A–Z and can be obtained in the form of a sizing card, a ring set of 26, or a set of 52 with ½ sizes.

4 Doming block Usually brass and available in different sizes, the most useful being a 5cm cube. This is used for making domes and semicircles of silver. It should be kept clean and dry. Any specks lying in the bottom of the block will mark the silver. The diameter of the silver should be slightly less than that of the dome hole.

5 Anvil or flatplate Either of these tools is useful when you are flattening or hammering silver. The size does not really matter, but the surface should be kept smooth, clean, and dry.

6 Arkansas stone You will need to keep your gravers, scorpers, and tips sharp. Keep the stone well oiled when you are using it so that loose particles do not become embedded in the tool being sharpened.

7 Large files You will need oval, flat, and half-round files.

8 Drawplates These steel plates have graduated holes, which are used to reduce the diameter or outline of round or sectional wire and tube.

9 Top cutters/side cutters These are useful for cutting up small paillons of solder, for cutting wire, and for getting into small difficult places.

10 Pliers You will eventually find that you will need several types of pliers. *Half-round pliers* can be used to bend metal into curves without marking the outside. *Parallel pliers* will grip a piece of silver equally along its length. *Snipe pliers* can be used in the same way as flat-nose pliers, but they can reach into difficult places. *Serrated pliers* are useful for gripping ends of wire when you need to pull it through the drawplate or straighten it in a vice. The serrations will mark the silver.

11 Crucible You will need a crucible to melt scrap and pour it into an ingot mold.

12 Scribe or scriber This little tool is used for marking a pattern on the silver, and for marking lines and circle centers. It should be kept clean and with a good point.

13 Drills Use an ordinary *hand drill* to make large holes. When you need to make small holes, use a *bow drill,* which allows you to hold your work with one hand while the drill is operated with the other. Wind the string around the shaft by twisting the top, and then, with the wooden handle held securely between two fingers, push the drill down. Allow it to rise, which it does because of the tension on the string, then push it down again. You can make fine *drill bits* from sewing needles, which are broken in half. Rub two opposite faces flat on your Arkansas stone (whetstone), and then rub off the other two corners. Small *hand*

vises or *drills,* which can be used with one hand, are available with different-sized chucks, which will take drills of minute size.

14 Metal punches Used in conjunction with the doming block, metal punches have all of the uses of wooden punches, but are harder and more precise.

15 Swage block This can be used with the handles of your metal punch to shape a strip of silver into a "U." The silver should be slightly narrower than the slot into which it is being punched.

16 Burnisher Burnishers are used for rubbing and polishing your finished work. They are also used for setting stones, by rubbing the silver over the stone. They should be kept dry and polished.

17 Suede stick and emery stick Both are used for cleaning and finishing. The emery stick should be used first, and it is possible to dissolve polish onto a suede stick with lighter fluid.

18 Sandbag This provides a good supportive base for silver when it is being shaped with either wooden or metal punches, or as a support when engraving.

19 Ring clamp and hand vise A ring clamp can be adjusted by means of a wedge to accommodate a ring of any size, and it will also support your work while you are working. The shank of a ring can be held in the protected jaws of the hand vise while you work on a setting.

20 Jointing tool This tool is used to hold chenier and wire straight while it is cut with a piercing saw.

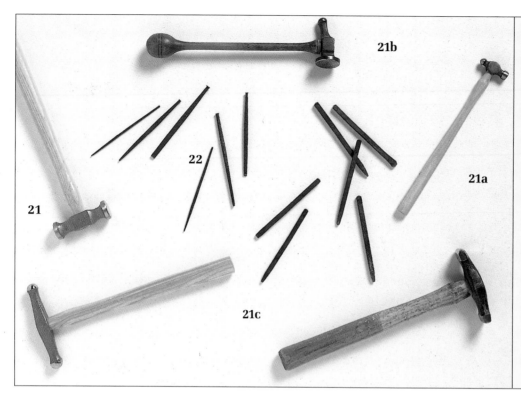

KEY:

21a Jeweler's hammer
21b Chasing hammer
21c Raising hammers
21 Planishing hammer
22 Punches and chasing tools
23 Pitch bowl
24 Drawing materials

21 Hammers A selection of hammers will be useful. A *jeweler's hammer* can be used to tap soft and thin silver. A *chasing hammer* should be used to strike the heads of repoussé and chasing tools. This type of hammer has a broad head and a rounded handle so that you can deliver rhythmic strokes. A *raising hammer* has a round nose, which is used to compress silver, while the flat face is used to extend the metal. Gentle taps with a *planishing hammer* will allow you to remove marks made by your raising or ball-peen hammer.

22 Punches and chasing tools These are used for shaping and marking silver. They can be bought in sets, or you can make them from square or round steel stock, tempered and ground or filed to shape. Keep your punches clean and dry.

23 Pitch bowl Pitch is used to hold your work firm when you are shaping, engraving, setting stones, chasing and doing repoussé work.

It is made from a mixture of asphaltum, plaster of Paris or pumice powder, and tallow or linseed oil. To make a stiffer pitch, add more plaster of Paris; to keep it soft, add more tallow or linseed. Pitch can be removed by being burnt, when it forms ash, or by being dissolved in turpentine. The bowl rests in a round wooden ring to keep it steady in all angles.

24 Drawing materials Set aside an area of your workroom for drawing materials and equipment. Keep a good supply of sharp pencils, tracing paper, drawing pads and erasers. You will also find dividers, compasses, a steel ruler, a calculator, templates (circles, curves, rectangles, and squares), a micrometer, a steel square, and a craft knife invaluable.

A pair of dividers and a steel ruler marked in inches and centimeters are invaluable to your work.

Soldering Equipment

A wide variety of different pieces of equipment is available for producing the heat needed during the manufacture of jewelry. Listed here are just a few of the torches and their gas supplies.

You will need to set aside an area on your workbench for soldering. If you are right handed, try the area on your left, because you will find it more convenient and practical to have your files, drills, vises, and so on on your right. If you are left handed, do the opposite. Alternatively, find a completely separate area for your soldering – one in which flames and acids will not threaten your other tools. If you do solder on the bench, make sure that the torch is readily at hand and insert a hook to hang it on. To guard against accidental burning, protect your soldering area with a heat-resistant mat, an old roasting pan or a revolving soldering stand. You will also need a charcoal block or synthetic soldering block. A charcoal block helps the work heat up quickly, but will burn through quickly if it is left to smolder. A soldering block is particularly useful when large work is heated because it does not burn through. However, soldering takes a little longer as the block does not reflect the heat.

Keep a good supply of paint brushes, old toothbrushes, empty jars, and an assortment of heat-resistant dishes handy in your workshop. They are always useful for cleaning, pickling, applying borax, and many other things! Keep a lighter close to your soldering torch.

After heating silver, it is usual to "quench" it. For this you need a 10:1 solution of water and sulfuric acid. This can be purchased ready mixed in the form of pickling powder, or you can buy pure sulfuric acid and prepare your own solution.

Use a glass measuring cup so that you can gauge the correct amount of acid. Wear good-quality rubber gloves and a heavy apron or smock.

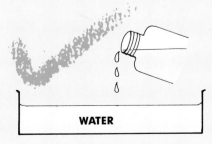

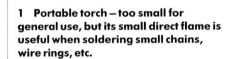

1   Portable torch – too small for general use, but its small direct flame is useful when soldering small chains, wire rings, etc.

2   Adjustable torch – the gas can come either from the main supply or a propane gas canister. The air is introduced by blowing down a flexible rubber pipe attached to the torch at point "a." It is a very good multi-purpose torch, but not suitable for very large pieces or prolonged high temperatures.

CAUTION
All acids are dangerous and must be handled and stored carefully. When making your "pickle," add acid to water; never add water to acid.

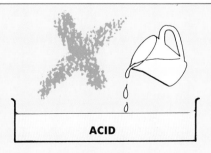

WATER

ACID

Add acid to water

Never add water to acid

Large Equipment

All the items of equipment listed here are expensive, and it may take you several years to acquire them all. Only consider purchasing these items when they are absolutely necessary, because some of the work they do can be done very satisfactorily by hand. However, I have listed them all to give you some idea of their uses and desirability.

1 Ultrasonic cleaner A stainless steel container is used with an ammonia-based detergent to remove, ultrasonically, excess polish from silver, gold, copper, or brass. The work is placed in a rack or on a hook so that it is suspended in the cleaning fluid, through

1

2

2a

2b

2c

which the sound waves penetrate. Although this is a very efficient cleaning method, patience, hot water, a toothbrush, and detergent will do just as well.

2 Polisher This is basically an electric motor with arms, to which can be attached a variety of buffing wheels, brushes, and polishes. It can be made by adapting a washing-machine motor, but a minimum of 1800 rpm is necessary for good results. Essential if you want a highly polished finish. Some are shown below: (2a) Rouge, (2b) Hyfin, and (2c) Tripoli. The strings (2e) are used for hand polishing.

3 Rolling mill Rolling mills come in a variety of sizes – and prices. Choose the best one you can afford. They are used for reducing the thickness of silver and of sectional and round wire. If you order

materials to your precise requirements, you will not need a mill. Use only silver, copper, gold, or brass in your mill: steel will leave dents and pits on the rollers, which will then have to be replaced professionally.

3

2d

2e

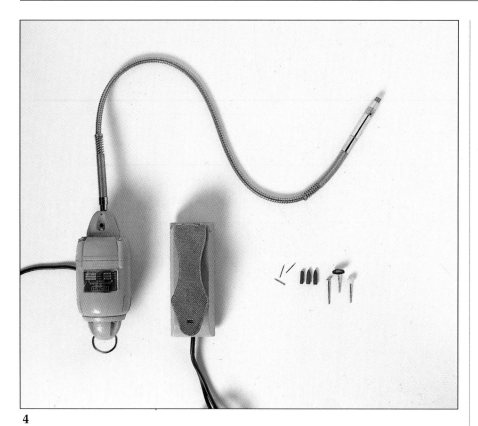

4

4 Flexible shaft machine This can be very useful. A variety of heads allows you to drill and texture surfaces, to remove solder, to clean inside rings and castings, to polish small areas, and to open out settings.

5 Scales All sorts of scales are available, ranging from hand-held ones to electronic ones. As long as they are accurate for very small weights, they will be suitable. You might be able to buy a secondhand set.

6 Kiln Kilns, which are either gas-fired or electric, are used for enameling, annealing, and casting. The same kiln should not be used for both enameling and casting, because the burnt-out residues from casting would contaminate the enamel, but annealing may be done in either.

5

6

7 Tumbler/polisher This useful piece of equipment is used for finishing fine work such as chains or rings. It is not suitable for large, flat areas. It consists of a rubber barrel about one-third full of small stainless steel shapes which, when water and special soap flakes are added, burnish the silver. The barrel is turned by a motor, which turns two spindles, and it can be left turning for several hours.

8 Stakes A variety of stakes can be used for shaping and raising larger pieces of silver if you are making spoons, bowls, or plates. They should be kept well polished and dry. These are necessary only if you want to concentrate on silver-smithing.

7

8

Chemicals

Listed here are some of the acids, cleaning and polishing materials, and other items that you will need. All acids and chemicals **must** be stored in a safe, dry, cool place. If children are likely to have access to your work area, you should install a cabinet that can be locked. When you are handling acids and chemicals, **always** work in a well-ventilated area and **always** wear protective clothing.

ACIDS

Nitric acid (HNO_3) is used for etching and, as a "bright dip," for removing fire stain. Use a solution of 3 parts water to 1 part acid. When you etch work, immerse the piece in the acid solution and "tickle" it with a feather from time to time to make sure the etch is uniform. Always keep an eye on your work so that it does not etch too quickly. To use nitric acid as a dip to remove fire stain, hang your work by a length of stainless steel wire for a couple of seconds in the solution. The cupric oxides will turn black or gray. Remove the work from the acid solution, rinse it under running water, and clean off the black with pumice powder and water. Repeat the process until all the oxides have gone. The acid will begin to attack the solder and silver, so you must immerse your work for only short periods.

Sulfuric acid (H_2SO_4) is used for pickling – that is, for removing oxides after heating – for removing burnt-on flux, and for removing grease. Use it in a solution of 10 parts water to 1 part acid.

ACETONE

This colorless, volatile, and highly flammable liquid is excellent for cleaning off grease and dirt, but it will leave a mark. It also dissolves many glues, so be careful where you use it. Always store it in a tightly closed container and use it only in a well-ventilated room.

SODA CRYSTALS

Approximately one spoonful of crystals in ½ gallon of boiling water will neutralize any residue of acid on your work after pickling. Soldering is impossible if there is any acid present, so it is often necessary to boil your work to remove all traces of acid. Rinse your work thoroughly in cold water.

ARGOTEC

This powder can be mixed with denatured alcohol or water to form a paste that can be painted onto your work before soldering to help prevent fire stain.

POTASSIUM SULFIDE

This is used to oxidize particular areas of work. Use one ½ inch cube of potassium sulfide in ½ gallon of hot water.

PUMICE POWDER

Keep a container of pumice powder and a toothbrush next to the sink. After soldering and pickling, a quick scrub with pumice and water will help to clean your work. Pumice is abrasive, so do not use it on polished work unless you want a matt finish.

STEEL WOOL

Rub steel wool gently over your finished work to give an interesting mat finish.

LIGHTER FLUID

Apply lighter fluid to a chamois leather, dustcloth, buffing cone, or polishing strings before you rub polish on. Hold the leather, dustcloth, or strings in a vice, and pull tight before you begin to rub.

JEWELER'S WAX

This can be used to hold your work while you set stones or engrave it. The wax can be melted on a flat piece of wood and held in a vice.

WET AND DRY PAPERS

Keep a selection of sandpaper from numbers 220 to 1200.

Soda crystals   Argotec   Potassium sulfide   Pumice powder

Nitric acid   Sulfuric acid   Acetone

Transferring Your Design

When you transfer your design, try to use the silver as economically as possible. For example, if your design has a straight edge, use the straight edge of the silver; if you are cutting out more than one piece, do not leave a large space between them, but try to fit them close together.

There are several ways in which you can transfer your design to the silver. Try them all until you find the one that suits you best. Of course, if the pattern or design is very simple, you can draw or scribe it directly onto the silver.

YOU WILL NEED

Silver
Modeling clay or eraser
Tracing paper
Sheet of acetate or carbon paper
Soft pencil with no eraser tip
Scribe
Masking tape
Adhesive – either spray glue or a glue stick

USING ACETATE

Rub the surface of the silver with a piece of modeling clay or an eraser. Lay a piece of acetate over your design and use a scribe to trace the pattern onto the acetate. Rub soft pencil into the scribed lines, then lay the acetate, scribed side down, on the silver, securing it with masking tape. Use the blunt end of the pencil to rub over the acetate so that the lines are transferred to the silver.

Remember that your design will appear in reverse if you do this. This may not matter with some designs – a symmetrical pattern will look the same whichever way it is traced – or you could turn the silver over after piercing. However, if you prefer, you can transfer your pattern to tracing paper and turn that over before tracing the pattern onto the acetate.

USING CARBON PAPER

Rub the surface of the silver with a piece of modeling clay or an eraser. Transfer your design to tracing paper and attach a piece of carbon paper to the silver, holding it in place with masking tape. Secure the tracing paper in place over the carbon paper and draw over the design, using a fine, hard point. Remove the tracing paper and the carbon. Use a scribe to go over the lines of your design, making sure that you do not accidentally smudge or wipe off the carbon lines as you work. When you have scribed over the whole design, wipe away any carbon marks that remain.

USING TRACING PAPER

Transfer your design to a piece of tracing paper. Cover the back of the tracing paper with spray adhesive or adhesive from a glue stick and leave it to dry for a few seconds. Place the tracing paper over the silver and press it firmly into position. Make sure that the paper is securely attached to the silver, then pierce or cut out your design. Peel away the remains of the tracing paper from the silver when you have finished. Any remaining paper can be removed with absorbent cotton soaked in acetate.

a
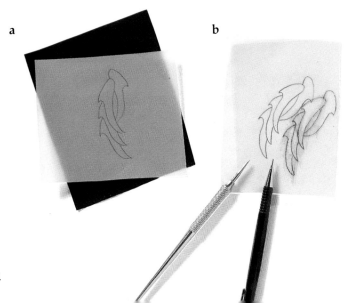

b

c

The design is: a) traced through carbon; b) traced through acetate;
c) tracing paper glued onto the silver before piercing.

Sawing and Piercing

When you cut out silver with a jeweler's saw, the blade will cut only on the down stroke. You should try to develop an easy, rhythmic action and never force the blade. When the blade gets stuck, lift up your work and let the saw find its natural position. You will then be able to continue.

Saw blades are available in sizes 4/0 (finest) up to 14. For most jewelry purposes numbers 4/0 to 4 will give an adequate range, and number 1/0 is probably a good one to start with.

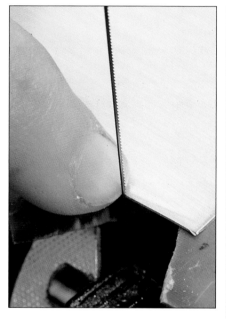

FITTING A BLADE
Take a number 1 blade, with the teeth of the blade toward you and pointing down, and slot the top end of the blade into the top fastening of your saw. Tighten the screw. Push the top end of the saw against the bench and slot the bottom end of the blade into the lower fastening of the saw. Tighten the screw. The blade should be firm and springy, with the teeth pointing down toward the handle.

CUTTING
Hold the saw at an angle of 90° to your work. Make the first cut, just touching the blade against your index finger as a guide. Let the blade fall through the silver and continue with a steady up-and-down movement along the line of your pattern.

PIERCING AN ENCLOSED AREA
Drill a small hole in the piece you want to remove. Undo the bottom end of the saw and pass the blade through the hole. Fasten the blade in position again, making sure it is firm, and cut around the enclosed area.

YOU WILL NEED
Jeweler's saw
3 packets of blades, number 1/0
Silver
Small hand drill with a ⅟₅₀-inch bit

TURNING A CORNER
When you reach a corner, rub the smooth, back edge of the blade into the corner you wish to turn, gradually turning the saw frame until it is facing in the new direction. Do not try to move forward until the blade is in the correct position.

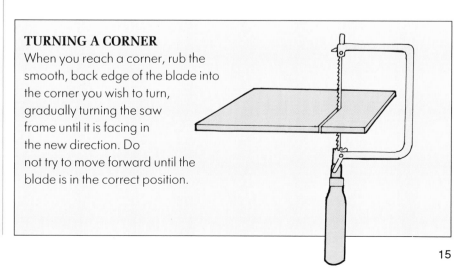

Annealing, Soldering, and Pickling

Silver needs to be annealed so that it is not too hard to work easily. When you start work on a new piece of silver, it is wise to anneal it after piercing to make sure it is soft before you start work. Silver needs re-annealing when it becomes work hardened, because if it is too hard it becomes brittle and is liable to crack.

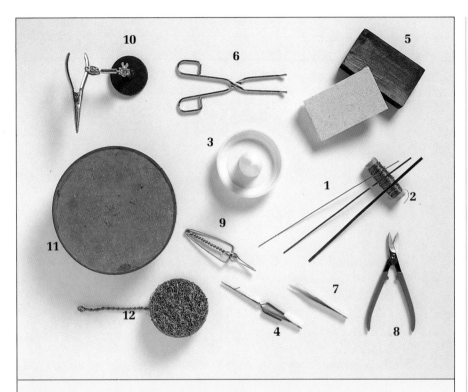

KEY:

1 Hard, medium, and easy solders
2 Binding wire
3 Flux or borax
4 Insulated tweezers
5 Charcoal block or soldering block
6 Brass tongs
7 Stainless steel tweezers
8 Snips
9 Spring tweezers
10 Third hand
11 Revolving soldering tray
12 Jeweler's wig

YOU WILL NEED

Hard, medium, and easy solders
Binding wire
Flux or borax
Insulated tweezers
Charcoal block or soldering block
Gas supply and torch
Pickle
Water
Brass tongs or tweezers
Paintbrush

ANNEALING

Make sure that the area in which you will be working is not in direct light. Put your silver on the soldering block and heat it with a soft flame – that is, in the pale blue area just behind the yellow tip. Feather the flame back and forth over the silver until it becomes a dull red. Keep the silver that color for a few seconds, then put out the flame. Quench the silver in the pickle, rinse in water, and dry.

SOLDERING

A flame with no added air.

A flame with added air, good for soldering.

A small, hard flame, good for soldering very small areas.

SOLDERING

Soldering is the process of permanently joining one piece of metal to another with heat, flux, and solder. It is often necessary to solder more than once on a piece of work, and there are several grades of solder available for doing this.

▌ Enameling, or IT, solder has the highest melting point; it is used only if the piece is to be enameled.

▌ Hard solder is generally the first solder to be used, and it is sometimes used three or four times on the same piece.

▌ Medium solder is used after hard solder. It does not always flow as easily, so cut it into small pieces.

▌ Easy solder is used after medium or hard. It is a good, flowing solder, which is often used for findings.

▌ Extra easy solder is very useful for low-temperature soldering.

Keep a divided dish near the soldering area for strips and paillons of hard, medium, and easy solder.

For practical purposes, only hard, medium, and easy solders are used for the projects described in this book.

Solder needs a catalyst or agent to make it flow. This is called flux or borax, and there are several different types of flux, some being more suitable for high-temperature soldering than others (see Gold, page 93). For most silver work, a borax cone in a dish or a liquid Auflux is suitable.

After fluxing the joint, apply the solder to your work. Apply the solder in small pieces called paillons. Cut two or three strips up the end of sheet solder using snips, and then cut across the strips to make small pieces. When you need thinner paillons, roll or hammer the ends of the solder first. Place the paillons in the borax dish so that they are coated in flux. Use the tip of a paintbrush to pick up the paillons and place them around the join or at the bottom of the joint for a ring because the solder will flow upward. Keep any spare paillons in separate small containers, marked "hard," "medium," or "easy."

Heat the work gently with a soft flame. As the water evaporates, the flux will start to bubble, but as soon as all the water has gone, it will settle down. Push any displaced solder back into position with your tweezers. Continue passing the flame over the work until it is heated and has turned cherry red. At about this point, the solder will flow, and a bright, shiny line will appear around the joint. Turn off the flame. Quench your work in the pickle, using brass tweezers to place it in and remove it from the acid. Rinse in cold water and dry.

If your work has other joints, you will need to use different solders. Use the same method as before, but replace the hard solder with medium, and then the medium solder with easy.

TO APPLY THE BORAX
Put a little water in the borax dish and rub the cone in a circular motion to produce a thickish paste. Use a fine paintbrush to apply the borax between the joint to be soldered.

BINDING WIRE
When a joint needs a little help to stay together during soldering, fasten binding wire around the work and tighten it by twisting the two ends with a pair of flat-nose pliers.

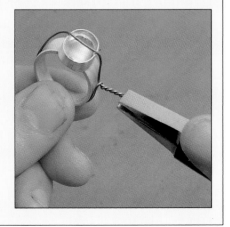

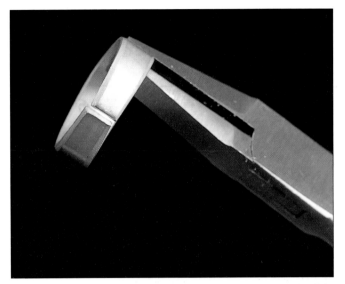

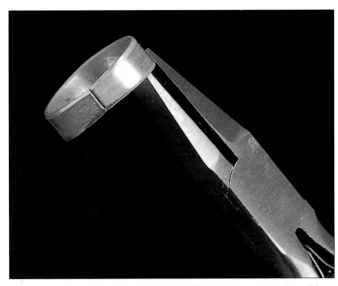

This join is not correctly aligned for soldering. Even if the solder did run, the join would need so much filing down that it would become very thin.

This join is correctly aligned which will, therefore, allow the solder to flow easily.

Solder will *not* run:
▌ If the join is not properly aligned and the gap is too large for the solder to jump.
▌ If the join is dirty, or if, after a previous attempt at soldering, there are traces of borax.

▌ If there is acid left in the joint.
▌ If the work is not hot enough.
▌ If the flame is too small for the amount of silver to be heated.

You can deliberately stop solder from flowing on a previously soldered area by painting the join with a paste of rouge powder and water. However, if the rouge paste has run into the area you want to solder, it won't work, so allow the rouged area to dry before fluxing the new joint.

On a large join which needs plenty of solder, you may find that a soldering stick is the best method.

Apply flux or borax in the usual way. Cut a long strip of solder and paint it with flux. Hold the solder in insulated soldering tweezers, then heat the work until it is cherry red. When the correct temperature is reached, feed the length of solder into the join, following the line just behind the flame. You can check that the temperature is correct by placing a paillon of the same solder you are using on the outside of the join. As you see it flow, apply the solder stick.

Solder is applied to a join using a soldering stick. Note how the paillon is in place to indicate flowing temperature.

When you need to solder a small piece to a large piece, apply flux and place the solder on the larger piece of work. Hold the smaller piece in soldering tweezers and paint a little flux on the bottom. Add a piece of the same solder and heat the small piece until the solder flows. Heat the large piece until the solder starts to run, and use the tweezers to place the small piece on the work, continuing to heat as you work. Remove the flame, holding the piece steady. Quench, rinse, and dry your work. Alternatively, paint flux onto both surfaces to be soldered. Place a small piece onto the large piece, and place paillons around the join. Gently heat the work from underneath or away from the small piece and, as the solder is about to run, bring the heat onto the small piece. Quench, rinse, and dry.

When soldering a small piece to a large piece, first heat the large area before allowing the solder to run.

It is sometimes necessary to alter the position of a finding or to remove a piece that has been soldered. To do this, attach the piece to the charcoal block with binding wire or hold it securely with tweezers. Apply flux to the joint you wish to undo and heat the work. As soon as the solder flows, lift up or reposition your work, using the soldering tweezers.

A finding is removed by unsoldering it from the silver sheet.

HOLDING

From time to time you will find it useful to have a "third hand" to help hold pieces while you are soldering. These tools are:

▌ Insulated soldering tweezers
▌ Wire tweezers
▌ Cotter pins
▌ Jeweler's wig
▌ Table with adjustable spring pliers.

PICKLING

While silver is being heated, it oxidizes and becomes black. When it is placed, still hot, in safety pickle or sulfuric solution, the oxides will disappear. If it is left for a few minutes, flux residues will disappear.

Take care when you are placing hot silver into an acid solution. The acid will spit and give off fumes, so make sure you are working in a well-ventilated area. Unfortunately, the spitting will inevitably cause holes in your clothes, so you should wear a heavy canvas or leather apron at all times in the workshop.

Pickling can be done the other way around. After soldering, quench the piece in water and then drop into a warm solution of sulfuric acid, and hold it at that temperature. This will clean the piece quite rapidly and bring the fine silver to the surface of the work. If it is not practical to pickle in warm acid, you can leave your work overnight in the acid. This will have similar results and is quite safe.

If any acid remains in your work after quenching and pickling, rinse it in water and boil the piece in a solution of hot water and a spoonful of soda crystals. Rinse and dry.

A hot silver piece is placed into the sulfuric acid. Note how the oxides have disappeared from the section that is immersed in the acid solution.

CAUTION

Remove any binding wire before immersing your work in the acid. The metal will contaminate the acid and turn everything pink. If that happens dispose of the acid – it is not possible to clean it. Remember: use only brass tweezers in acid.

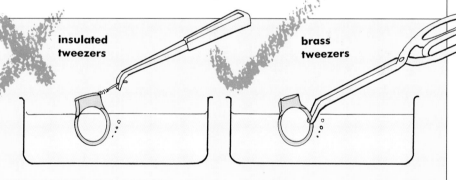

insulated tweezers

brass tweezers

REMOVING FIRE STAIN

Standard silver contains 7.5 percent copper, when it is heated in air, the copper on the surface oxidizes and leave a black mark on the polished silver. This can be removed in a variety of ways:

▌ File it off, taking care not to lose the shape of the work
▌ Rub a dampened "water of Ayr" stone over the mark to form a grayish paste. Keep rinsing the paste off to check that the stain has disappeared
▌ Before soldering, coat your work with Argotec mixed with water or denatured alcohol. Avoid painting this mixture into any solder joints because Argotec is basically a flux and would cause the solder to run. Pickle off after use
▌ Have your work silver plated.

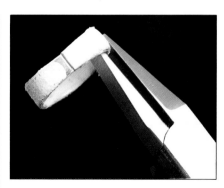

A ring ready for soldering, with a coating of "Argotec" to prevent fire staining.

Using Wire

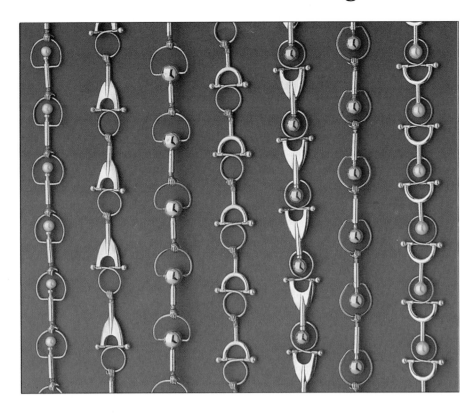

There are numerous uses for wire in jewelrymaking. It is supplied in a variety of sections:

○ Round

△ Triangular

⌓ Semicircular or D section

▢ Square

▭ Rectangular

⌐ Bearer

Wire with a hole through the center is known as chenier. It is available in round and square sections with walls of different thicknesses. Wire is supplied in coils by weight, and chenier comes in lengths. Wire and chenier can be drawn down to a smaller width by means of a suitable drawplate.

YOU WILL NEED

Copper and silver wire, 24 gauge–12 gauge
Round drawplate
Round-nose pliers
Half-round pliers
Flat-nose pliers
Hand drill and hook
Large serrated pliers
Vise

DRAWING DOWN WIRE

Drawing down D section wire.

1 File one end of a length of wire to a longish taper and then anneal it.

2 Find the size of hole in the drawplate that will take the taper, but not the full width of the wire, and push the taper through, gripping the end with the serrated pliers.

3 Pull the wire through the hole, keeping it straight. Continue working down through the holes annealing the wire as it becomes hard and difficult to work. Wire can be coaxed through the holes by rubbing a little wax along its length.

Hold the drawplate in the vise, but be careful not to close the jaws of the vise over any of the holes in the plate, which could burr or damage the fine edges.

PULLING CHENIER DOWN

1 Take a length of wire that is longer than the chenier and that has a diameter the same as the inside diameter of the chenier.

2 Coat the wire with wax and pull it through the chenier to coat the inside walls with wax.

3 Replace the wire in the chenier and file one end to a taper.

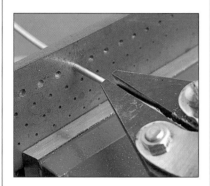

4 Pull the chenier through the drawplate as for wire, then remove the wire by pulling the protruding end of the wire through a hole in the drawplate that is too small for the chenier.

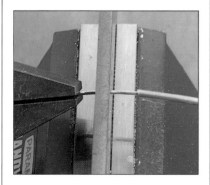

MAKING A JUMP RING

Jump rings are used for joining chains, loops, and catches. They are supplied in most sizes, or you could order a selection of sizes. They are also very easy to make yourself.

1 Take a former of the appropriate size – the wrong end of a drill bit will do – and anneal the wire.

2 Put the former in the vice so that it is horizontal, protecting the cutting edge if you are using a drill bit.

3 Close the vice and grip the end of the wire with serrated pliers.

4 Wrap the other end of the wire around the former so that each coil fits snugly against the previous one until the wire is finished. Take the former out of the vice.

5 Snip off any protruding ends of wire; wrap masking tape around the wire while it is still on the former.

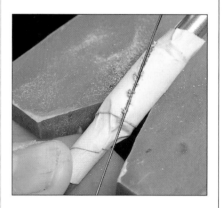

6 Pierce through the tape and wire, making a slightly diagonal line and taking care not to mark the former. Remove the tape.

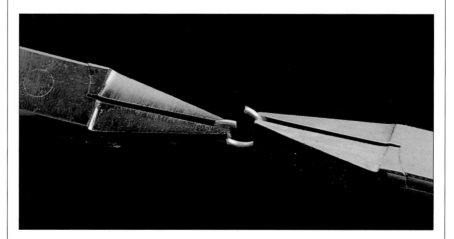

7 You can close the ends of a jump ring by taking a pair of flat-nose pliers in each hand. Hold the jump ring in one pair of pliers and use the other pair to adjust the other side of the jump ring with a twisting movement to close the ends together.

MAKING A BROOCH PIN

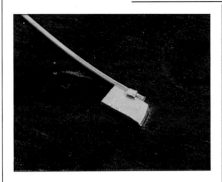

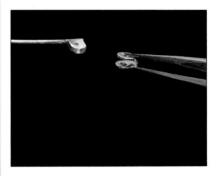

1 Make a silver tag from sheet silver; it should be slightly less thick than the inside of the fichu joint. Solder it to a length of 18 gauge round wire. File a groove along the top of the tag to make a good joint.

2 Use a jeweler's saw to cut the wire to size and file the end into a good point. Gently tap the wire with your jeweler's hammer while you roll it (as far as the tag) on a smooth metal surface. This hardens the pin after soldering.

3 Drill a hole through the tag to align with the holes of the fichu joint.

4 A pin can also be made by simply bending the wire. Do not anneal the wire – it will stay springy if it has not been heated.

TWISTING SILVER WIRE TOGETHER

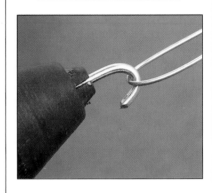

1 Take a piece of silver wire about 20 inches long and fold it in half.

2 Anchor the two ends in the vice and tighten it.

3 Take a hand drill and secure a hook in the chuck. Put the loop of silver wire over the hook and, keeping the wire taut, turn the drill until the wire is twisted as far as you want. Remove the wire from the hook and the vice.

4 Put flux along the length of twisted wire, place paillons along its length, or use a solder stick and solder it.

5 Try different combinations of wire. Use one length of copper and one of silver, or twist two smaller wires and then twist those with larger wires. Twist round wire with square wire. Try flattening the twisted wire, either with a hammer or through a rolling mill.

TWISTING WIRE

You can make fascinating combinations by twisting wires together. Wire will twist more evenly if it has been evenly annealed. You can either anneal the wire carefully with your torch or in a kiln at a temperature around 1100°–1200°F for a minute or two. Alternatively, you can buy soft annealed coils.

Twisted wire can be made into rings, loops for chains or earrings, used around the edge of a stone setting, or as general decoration. Experiment!

CHAINS

There are many different chains you can buy from your supplier. They are usually quite fine and, for general purposes, they are difficult to improve upon. However, if you want a chain with larger links or one that is more interesting, try making one yourself. It is important that chain should move freely, so try to make sure that the links are free to move in all directions.

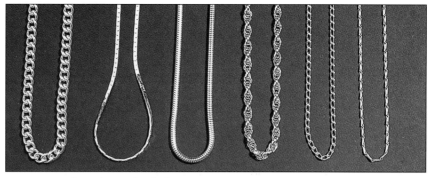

A selection of ready-made chains.

MAKING OVAL LINKS

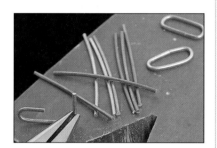

1 Cut several lengths of wire the same length – 1½ inches, for example – bend up the ends and solder them together. Make them round by sliding them over a mandrel or former and tapping them with a mallet.

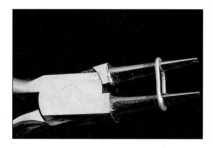

2 Take a pair of round-nose or flat-nose pliers. Place the loop over the plier ends, with the soldered joint at one end, and pull the pliers apart just enough to stretch the wire.

If you are making several links, mark the position on the pliers with tape or a red line so they are the same size.

MAKING RECTANGULAR LINKS

1 Cut several pieces of wire to length, allowing for the joints to be in the middle of the long sides. Use your dividers to mark each piece where the bends will be, then, with a triangular file, make a groove along the marked lines to slightly more than half the depth of the silver.

2 Carefully bend the wire with flat-nose pliers, apply flux, and hard solder up all the corners.

MAKING LITTLE BALLS

Silver bracelet. Rebecca Smith.

1 Cut equal lengths of silver wire, approximately ¹⁄₁₀-inch long, place them one at a time on your charcoal block, and heat them until they run up into a ball.

MAKING A CHAIN

To make a chain, pierce through the soldered joint of the links; open up the joint enough to link into the next link. Close the link using flat nose pliers. Isolate each link to resolder the joint.

Filing

To achieve a good finish on silver, every scratch that is made has to be removed and replaced by a finer one. Do this by working systematically from coarse files, to needle files, to wet and dry papers, to the different grades of polish. At each stage you should check that you have erased the scratches from the previous tool.

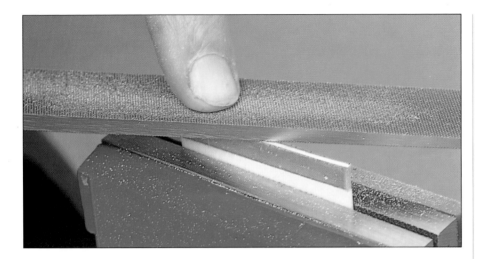

A file cuts in only one direction, and there are many different shaped files that will follow the line of your work. In general, use a flat file on a flat surface; an oval or half-round file on inside curves; a triangular file for grooves and small corners; a rectangular or square file for right angles; and a round file to cut "U" grooves and open out holes.

Some rectangular or flat files have a cutting edge, which is useful for making grooves, and some files have a safe edge, which allows you to file one surface without damaging another that is close to it.

FLAT FILING
When you are filing a long edge flat, hold the silver parallel in the safe jaws of the vice. Hold the flat file in one hand and move it diagonally in long smooth strokes along the silver, keeping it flat and straight with your index finger.

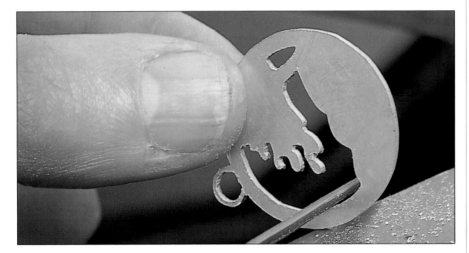

CURVES
On inside curves, use an oval or half-round file, keeping it straight. Work on alternate sides of the work to keep the filing even.

RIFFLER FILES
These files have curved tips and a smooth center that is used as the handle. They allow filing in difficult corners and on convex and concave surfaces.

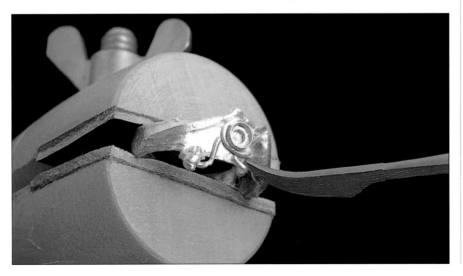

From top: flat filing; filing an inside curve; and using a riffler file.

Texturing

You can add an interesting further dimension to your work by texturing all or some of the surfaces. Before you start to texture, make sure that the surface is clean and free of grease. Some surfaces can be textured before piercing, but a simple mat or frosted finish is added after polishing.

PLANISHING

Support your work on a polished stake or wooden former, and work around the piece with your planishing hammer in a smooth rhythmic action. This should be done on your finished piece, because the gentle tapping will slightly mark the surface. Do not hit too hard or you could alter the shape of your work.

USING A PUNCH

You can make your own patterns to achieve an interesting effect on your work by filing grooves into the end of a punch. The reverse pattern will appear on your work.

To do this use steel stock, about 4 inches long and ¼ inch square, and slightly taper both ends with your file. File your pattern into one end. Finish the ends by beveling the corners so that the edges do not drag on your work. Harden the end by heating the punch to cherry red and quickly quenching in cold water. Reheat only the working end with a soft flame until it becomes yellow. Quench again. This method will allow you to produce a variety of different patterns yourself, although it is possible to buy different patterned punches.

To add texture with a punch: set your work by gently heating the pitch, dropping the work in it, and, when it is slightly cooler, pushing the pitch up around the edge of the work with your fingers. Dampen your fingertips first.

With your punch at an angle of 90° to your work, hit the top with a hammer and work it steadily around the area you want to mark. If the work starts to curl up out of the pitch, remove it, anneal and straighten it before replacing it in the pitch. When you have finished, gently heat the pitch around the work and use an old pair of pliers to prize up the edge of the work and lift it out. Pitch can be burned off or dissolved in turpentine.

FLEXIBLE-SHAFT MACHINE

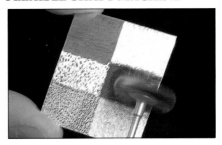

If you possess, or have access to, a flexible-shaft machine, there are all sorts of little burrs and cutters that can be used to produce different surfaces on silver. Try them out on a piece of scrap metal first to see what effect you prefer. It is also useful to get some practice with the tool before you start to texture a beautifully finished piece of work.

OTHER ABRADERS

Steel wool and wet and dry papers will give a good mat finish if they are rubbed over your finished work. Try them on scrap metal first to be sure of the effect. Use a circular motion or a back-and-forth movement. If you have a polishing motor, you can fit a stainless steel wheel, which also gives a mat finish.

Finishing and Polishing

Finishing work well will transform a rather dull-looking piece into something you will be proud of. The processes of polishing and finishing may take longer than you imagine, but if you complete each stage thoroughly, you will be well rewarded with the end result.

YOU WILL NEED

Some or all of the following:
Wet and dry papers
Polishing sticks
Chamois leather, dustcloths
Household silver polish
Polishing strings
Lighter fluid
Flexible-shaft machine with mops
    and brushes
Polishing motor with hard,
    medium and soft buffers
Cone for inside ring polishing

POLISHING BY HAND

An emery stick is used to give a sanded finish.

After completing the fine filing on your work, remove the filing marks by rubbing wet and dry papers over the surface. Begin with a fairly coarse paper – 240 or 400 – and work down to 600 and 1200, if necessary. As their name suggests, these papers can be used with or without water.

Make a polishing stick by gluing pieces of suede onto wooden sticks measuring approximately 12 × ¾ × ½ inch.

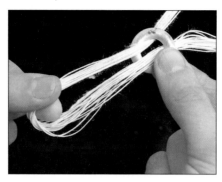

Polishing strings – use as many or as few as you need to reach difficult areas.

To polish inside difficult areas, keep some polishing strings hooked up in your workshop. Thread as many as necessary through the work and moisten them with lighter fluid, apply the polish, and rub the work along the string. The polishes required for both the sticks and the strings are:

▌ **Coarse** – Tripoli, which is a sticky brown block
▌ **Medium** – Hyfin, which is a finer white block
▌ **Fine** – rouge, which is a fine red round block.

Polishing on an electric motor.

Remove any thick polish left on the surface with detergent and warm water before moving on to the next grade of polish. You will find it useful to have a chamois leather, spread out on a large, flat surface. You can rub the polishes onto it with lighter fluid.

POLISHING BY MACHINE

You will need separate buffing wheels for each polish – a stiff brush for Tripoli, a softer brush or cotton buffer for Hyfin, and a wool buffer for rouge. Hard felt cones are used inside rings.

CAUTION
Before you use a polishing motor, make sure that you have tied long hair back and that you have no loose clothing that could get caught in the revolving wheel.

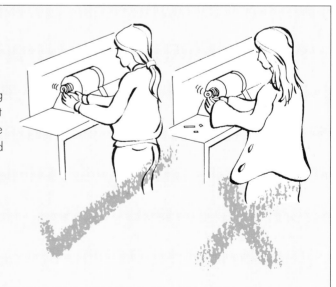

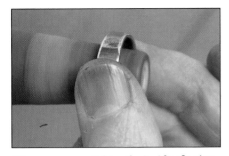

When you are polishing the inside of a ring on a felt cone, hold the ring firmly and rotate it so that all the inside edges come into contact with the cone.

With the motor running, press some polish onto the buffer. Then hold the work to be polished between 4 and 5 o'clock on the wheel. Do not place it above the center line of the wheel, or the speed will whip your work out of your hands, with possible disastrous consequences. Use both hands to hold the work and push it toward the wheel. If you push the edges too hard, they can very quickly lose their crispness.

After each application of polish, clean your work with detergent or in an ultrasonic cleaner.

To highlight edges or raised surfaces on a mat piece, rub them with a burnisher, using a little pressure. Remember to keep the burnisher polished to prevent it from scratching your work.

OXIDIZING

After you have polished your work, you may feel that an area would look good with a black background. This can be oxidized, using a small piece of potassium sulfide – a cube about $\frac{1}{2} \times \frac{1}{2} \times \frac{1}{2}$ inch dissolved in about 2 pints of boiling water. Immerse the piece in the liquid by hanging it from a piece of silver wire. Remove it after about a minute when it is a good black color. The color varies according to the time the item is immersed, and if the solution is too hot, flaking may result. You can now polish away any surface you have designed for highlights, but be careful if you are using a polishing buffer not to remove the oxidized background. A burnisher can be used more selectively.

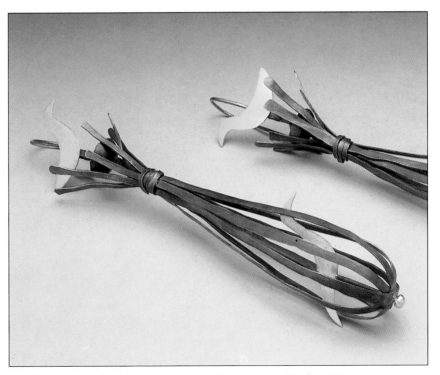

Oxidized silver with gold decoration. Brooch and earrings. Daphne Krinos.

Findings

Findings is the word used to describe the mechanical fittings that are attached to jewelry and that hold the piece on the body or attach it to your clothing. Standard silver findings should always be used when you work with silver. Silver plate on base metals can soon wear away and may cause allergy problems. Manufacturer's catalogues include a good choice of findings, but you will sometimes find it more appropriate to make your own. Always take care to position your findings so that your work is balanced correctly.

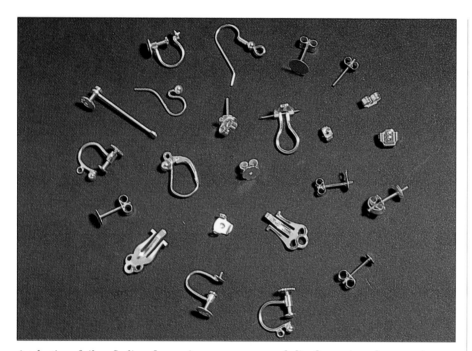

A manufactured clip fitting.

A selection of silver findings for earrings – ear screws and clips for unpierced ears, and ear hooks and wires with butterfly fittings for pierced ears.

UNPIERCED EARS

If you are making earrings for unpierced ears, it is probably easier to buy fittings for clips or screw-type fittings. It is possible to pierce the shape from sheet silver if you need a heavier gauge, and then wire can be bent to fit.

EARRINGS

You can make earrings in several styles:
▮ Wire with butterfly fitting
▮ Wire hooks
▮ Hoops
▮ Clips.

PIERCED EARS

Cut pieces of round wire approximately ½ inch long, file one end straight across, and use easy solder to solder them to the earring. Taper the other end and, about one-third of the way up the pin, file a tiny groove around the diameter. Burnish the pin after rolling it along a metal surface, gently hammering to harden the silver. Add butterfly fittings.

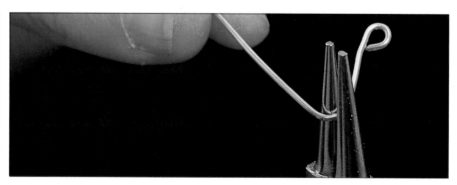

A wire is bent for ear loops.

To make loop earrings for pierced ears, bend up loops of wire using round or half-round pliers. Avoid soldering if possible, but if it is necessary, solder before bending and harden by tapping with the hammer as above.

To make hoops solder a 20-gauge wire to the end of thicker wire, and drill a hole the same size in the other end. Wrap the wire around the top of a mandrel and hit downward until the hoop is springy and the correct size.

PINS AND BROOCHES

There is a large selection of brooch fittings you can buy. Some of these are very small, and it may be more appropriate to make your own. Making brooch pins is described in the section on wire. You can make your own catch by bending a piece of wire, of which you have tapered one end, and flattening the end that is to be soldered to the work. Make a fichu joint by cutting out a rectangle of silver approximately ¾ × ¼ inch, filing two grooves at ¼ and ¾ inch, and bending it up with flat-nose pliers. Run hard solder up the grooves before soldering it to your work with easy solder.

CUFFLINKS

Attachment for chain to link onto a cuff-link.

To make a chain link fitting, solder a half-round, using wire or piercing it out from a sheet, to the back of the cufflink and attach five links of chain that you have made or belcher chain. Then attach that to the opposite side of the link. You can combine a T-bar with a chain by attaching the chain to

A T-bar fitting – the "V" is soldered into position, and the bar then riveted onto it.

a piece of thick round wire or chenier.

To fix a T-bar, solder the "U" or "V" shape at an angle to the link and attach the T-bar by means of a rivet after the soldering is completed.

NECKLACES, BRACELETS, AND PENDANTS

Bolt ring.

The clasps you will use are:
- Bolt ring
- Box catch

- Hook and eye
- Spring fitting

- Riveted joint.

Bolt rings are the usual way of fastening manufactured chains. They come in different sizes and work well. After soldering, leave to air-cool, as the spring will become soft if it is quenched immediately.

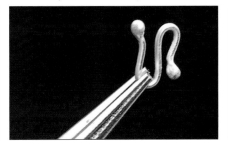

Wire for hook with both ends run up to make little balls.

A hook and eye fastening gives the greatest scope for your own creativity. A simple style can be made by heating both ends of a length of 18-gauge wire, approximately 1½ inches long, so that the ends run up into balls. Hold the wire in your insulated tweezers, flux the ends, and concentrate the flame on one end, with a charcoal block behind it. The end will run up into a ball as it begins to melt. Turn it over and repeat the process on the other end. Use round and half-round pliers to bend the wire into a long "S" shape. Solder up one end with easy solder, and curl the ball on the other end to turn up. Hammer the central area flatter on the anvil to

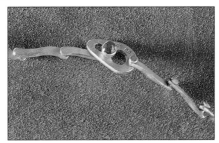

A sapphire was set into the end of this fastener to add interest to the back of the necklace.

harden it up and improve the appearance.

Another way of achieving the same end is to pierce out an end tag, with a hole at the chain end going into a slit. Make the fastener by bending up a piece of wire the same diameter as the slit and soldering a silver ball to the top so that it will fit through the opposite hole.

Riveting

Silver can be joined together by means of a rivet. This is often useful if you are using other materials – wood, for example – which cannot be soldered.

Drill two holes of $\frac{1}{10}$ inch into silver 1.
Mark the position for holes on the wood 2 and silver 3, and drill.
Solder in two silver wires to fit the holes in silver 1.
Countersink the top of the holes in silver 3.
Place pieces 2 and 3 over the silver wires. Push down.
Cut wires close to 3 and file flat.
Support the underside of 1 on the anvil.
Using a pointed punch, spread the tops of the wire pins by tapping gently a couple of times with a small hammer.
Take a flat-headed punch and continue to spread the top until it is firm. Finish neatly off with a file.

Drill through silver 4, wood 5, and silver 6 with a $\frac{1}{16}$-inch drill bit.
Take a length of annealed wire which fits snugly through the holes.
Cut each end of wire so that it protrudes fractionally beyond silver pieces 4 and 6.
Countersink the holes at a and b.
Push both wires through all three thicknesses.
Support the end of the wire on the anvil.
Spread the head of the wire with a punch.
Turn it over and spread the other side.
File to finish and clean with an emery cloth.

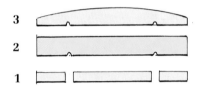

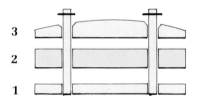

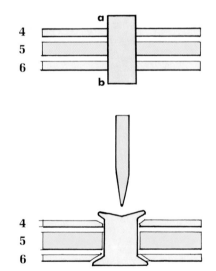

You should be able to file and polish the heads so that they disappear. If the head of the rivet is well spread, it will sit inside the countersink and be quite safe.

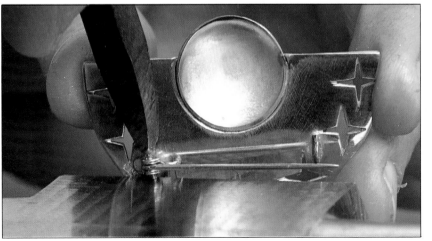

Doming and Shaping

Being able to shape your silver into round domes and "U" shapes gives an added depth to your work. A doming block is used for forming a disk of silver sheet into a dome or semisphere. A swage block is used for forming a strip of silver sheet into a U-shaped section. A sandbag is used to support the silver while it is being shaped with wooden or metal formers or punches. A lead block will give under the pressure of a punch, but will retain the shape around it. Lead bits, if heated with silver, will result in disastrous holes, so always put paper or muslin between silver and lead.

MAKING A DOME

YOU WILL NEED

Doming block
Wooden or steel punches
Sandbag
Swage block
Hammer

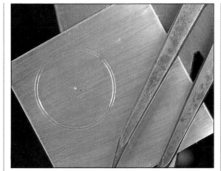

1 Cut a disk of silver. When you are piercing out a disk, mark the circle on the silver and then mark another circle about 1/10 inch larger around it, pierce between the two lines, and then file down to the first line.

2 Anneal the silver, then place it in the appropriate semisphere in the block. The disk should be slightly smaller than the diameter of the semisphere. With a punch to fit, hammer the silver into the semisphere. Make the dome as small as you need, annealing it when necessary.

MAKING A "U" SECTION

1 Lay a strip of silver down the largest groove of the swage block. Make sure that the silver is not wider than the groove.

2 Lay the side of an appropriate punch along the silver and hammer the punch with a wooden mallet to push the silver into the groove. Do not use a metal hammer, which will mark the punch.

Other Materials

With a little inspiration, all sorts of interesting and inexpensive jewelry can be made by combining a variety of different materials with silver. Keep a collection of bits and pieces to experiment with in spare moments.

Turned walnut bowl with fine silver decoration. The silver is attached to the wood with rivets. Jinks McGrath and Steve Turner.

Rosewood and silver bangle with matching ring. Jinks McGrath.

WOOD

Hardwoods are the most suitable to use with silver. There are, of course, sound environmental reasons for not using any hardwood in jewelry making, but it is possible to find wood such as ebony, which can be reclaimed from an old mirror or hairbrush. Boxwood, which grows readily, is an excellent light-colored close-grained wood, as are lignum vitae (guaiacum), although it is rather oily, and rosewood. Wood can be attached with rivets, screws, or a good-quality glue. It can be pierced out using your jeweler's saw with one of the heavier blades, but you might find a coping saw easier on a large job. Edges can be filed and sanded, and rubbing beeswax or linseed oil over a finished piece will bring it to life.

Another way of using wood is to collect the dust produced by filing and sanding and mixing it into epoxy resin. You can build up an image with different colors by filling the spaces between silver wires soldered to a framework with the wood and resin mixture. Leave it to dry, level off with a file, and then sand until smooth. Any little holes can be filled with more resin mixture. Finally, oil the surface.

NATURAL STONE

A walk on the beach or in the country or a gentle stroll in a park can be not only a source of inspiration, but also an excellent source of natural stone. Some stones and pebbles will be harder and more durable than others, so try flaking and breaking them first to see whether they are worth using. Interesting pieces can be mounted in silver or wrapped in silver wire and then linked up to make an attractive pattern within the overall piece. Alternatively, you can buy wonderful ready-cut pieces of agate from lapidary dealers, who often also offer unusual shapes, which can be used to make intriguing jewelry.

PAPIER-MÂCHÉ

Make little papier-mâché balls or ovals, paint them, give them a coat of varnish, and drill through the middle so they can be hung on necklaces or earrings.

A finely painted ball hung on silk threads. Paul Vincent.

ACRYLICS

Plexiglass sheets can be bought in a variety of thicknesses and colors, and companies that make or use large quantities of plastic can be generous with their scraps. Use a coping saw for most of the cutting, as the heat that is generated will soon clog a small jeweler's saw blade. Plexiglass can be filed, sanded, polished, and buffed with metal polishes. It can be set into silver, riveted, and screwed, but a special plastic glue should be used, as most ordinary adhesives alter the surface of the acrylic. Plexiglass can be heated in a warm oven (about 200°) and bent to shape. Be careful not to overheat, which will cause air bubbles within the plastic. Resins are used for cold-cast enameling. Colors are mixed with the resin and a catalyst, and the liquid is poured into depressions or cells in the silver. If you are casting resin into a framework that does not have a metal back, place the frame on an oiled tray or mold.

GLASS

Clear glass or pebbles can be used as the basis for colorful painted designs. Use enamel paints and cover them with a coat of protective varnish. You can make a very original necklace by collecting interesting shapes and holding them in a silver framework. Small pieces of colored glass can be inlaid and glued into silver cells to build up a mosaic, or use glass beads, mixed in with silver beads, to make attractive earrings and necklaces.

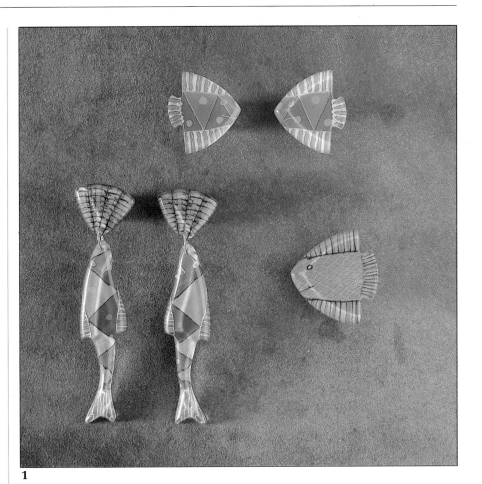

1

1 Cast acrylic on top of a painted base makes these pieces very colorful. Rowena Park.

2 Little paintings on clear glass joined with silver wire and tiny beads. Nancy Church.

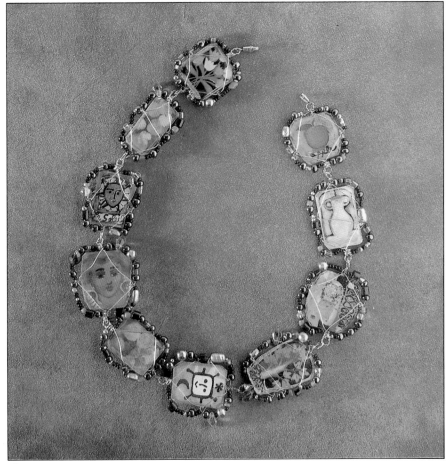

2

FINDINGS

Findings for use with other materials are much the same as those already described for use with silver. Most will have to be glued or riveted in position, but if possible design your piece so that the fitting can be soldered to the silver sheet first.

NECKLACE THREAD

For a flexible necklace made of different materials, thread is often used instead of wire or chain.

Silk thread is used for stringing pearls, freshwater pearls, and semiprecious beads. The drilled pearls or beads are threaded onto silk strands with a fine needle made from a very fine brass wire, doubled and twisted together. After each pearl is added, make a knot in the silk to prevent them from wearing each other away and from all falling off if the threads break. The silk is joined to the catch at the back by threading a fine spring ring over the threads and through the jump ring on the catch; this prevents wear at the point of contact. The silk is then threaded back through the last three or four pearls and knotted again. The knot is coated with transparent glue and made as small as possible so that it does not impede the flow of the pearls.

Nylon is used for threading other beads as long as they are not too heavy. The nylon is knotted at the ends only and held in little findings called crimp beads, which close down over the glued and knotted end of the nylon. The crimp beads are then linked to the fasteners. Alternatively, the nylon threads can be knotted directly onto the fastener.

Leather thread is used for very large beads. Tie the ends together with a bow or knot or fit a coiled loop over the ends.

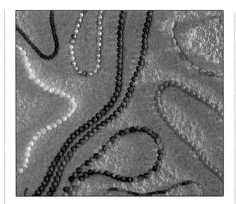

A selection of colorful and semiprecious beads. Marcia Lanyon.

Tiger tail (very strong thread) is a stronger, but less flexible, way of hanging beads. It has the advantage that it will not lose its shape. It cannot be knotted, so it is looped at both ends, and the loop is kept in place by means of a crimp bead. The loose ends of the thread are then tucked back through the beads. The fastener is attached to the tiger tail loop. If the beads are not heavy enough for tiger tail, it may kink.

TITANIUM

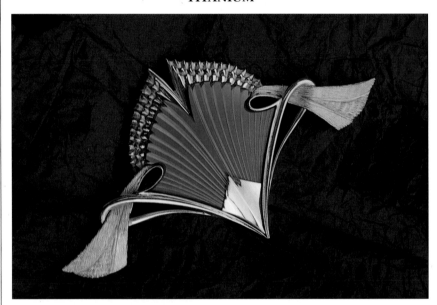

Colored titanium set into a brooch. Brian Eburah.

This light, gray metal, which is extremely strong, is used in jewelry mainly because of the attractive range of colors that appear after heat treatment. Because it is so hard, piercing should be done with a strong blade, and it takes longer than piercing silver. Titanium should not be rolled down in your rolling mill, and it cannot be soldered, shaped, or forged. It is, therefore, either set like a stone into, or riveted onto, a piece of work. Before heating titanium, clean the surface by rubbing it with wet and wet dry papers and degreasing it with an ammonia-based detergent. Small particles of titanium are combustible, so do not file, saw, or clean it near a naked flame.

Heat can be applied with a torch all over a piece or concentrated locally to produce a spectacular range of colors. After heating, titanium should be left in the air to cool. The colors will remain: they appear as a result of the film of oxides, produced by the heat, on the surface. Light passes through the film and is then refracted from the surface of the metal to produce all colors of the spectrum. After coloring, designs or lines can be scribed with a diamond-tipped scribe.

Simple Rub-over Stone Settings

A piece of jewelry can be greatly enhanced by the addition of a well-chosen stone. There are many ways of setting stones to show them off to their best advantage – large, opaque stones look best with a simple rub-over setting, for example, and most faceted stones (those with flat-polished faces) are enhanced by an open-back setting which allows the light to reflect around the stone. When you use a stone or stones, try to design a piece around them. Carefully consider the sort of setting you need and work with that in mind. Some stones are softer than others and are best set so that they are not constantly vulnerable. Lapidary dealers have a host of stones to choose from, so have a good look before you make your selection.

YOU WILL NEED

Silver sheet
Bearer wire
Small flat punch
Hammer
Setter's wax
Ring vise
Burnisher
Suede stick
Round and half-round pliers
Mandrel
Graver
Divider

RUB-OVER SETTING FOR ROUND STONES

Measure the diameter of your stone – ½ inch, for example – and use the calculation $2\pi r$ to find the circumference of the stone ($\pi = \frac{22}{7}$ or 3.141): $2 \times \frac{22}{7} \times .25 = 1.5 = 1\frac{1}{2}$ inches

The silver band surrounding the stone is known as a bezel. Choose a thickness of silver that is appropriate to the size of the stone to make the bezel. Generally, use the thinnest silver that is practicable. Silver that is too thick can detract from the stone and can be hard to push over. In this case, if the stone has a diameter of ½ inch, a thickness of about ⅛ inch is right. To find the length of the bezel, add together the circumference of the stone and 1½ times the thickness of the silver:

$$1\frac{1}{2} + (\frac{1}{8} \times 1.5) =$$
$$1\frac{1}{2} + \frac{3}{16} = 1\frac{11}{16} \text{ inches}$$

1 Measure the height with a pair of dividers. Mark this height on your silver by laying the dividers on a straight edge of the silver and running them along the surface.

2 Mark out the length you need, making sure that both ends are square. Pierce out the silver and anneal it. With your half-round pliers, bend the two ends up so that they meet exactly. At this stage there is no need to make the shape round. To keep the shape tight for soldering, push the two ends past each other and then spring them back into position. Solder the ends together using hard solder.

3 Make the bezel round by tapping it on your mandrel or in your pliers. File off any excess solder from the inside.

4 Check that the stone fits. It should not be necessary to force the stone to fit; it should just slip in. A small gap all round is acceptable. If the bezel is too small, pierce it open at the solder

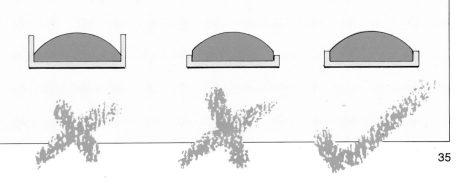

STONE SETTING
The height of the bezel should be about one-third the height of the stone. However, look at the stone and note where the curve actually starts, for this is where your bezel should rest to hold the stone down.

seam and add a piece of the same silver used for the bezel. Solder it up again. If the bezel is too big, pierce it open at the solder seam, cut out a piece and try the stone. Resolder the joint.

5 Rub the bottom of the bezel on a flat file to make sure it sits perfectly straight, then place the bezel on a piece of silver between $\frac{1}{32}$ and $\frac{1}{16}$ inch thick. Flux the silver and solder it. You can use medium solder, but if you have much more soldering to do on your piece, it may be better to use hard solder. Place the paillons around the outside edge of the bezel and heat the surrounding silver before applying heat to the bezel.

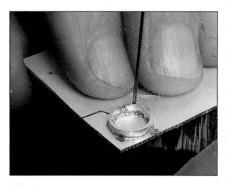

6 After pickling and rinsing, cut away the excess silver from the outside of the bezel. File the outside edge and clean it with wet and dry papers. The bezel is now ready to add to your piece.

7 If you need an open setting so that the light brings out the best qualities in your stone, cut away most of the back. Place one side of the dividers on the outside of your setting and the other side inside the bezel. Scribe a line around the

circumference, leaving a margin of about $\frac{1}{16}$ inch of silver on the inside. Drill a hole in the center of the setting and pierce up to the line to cut away the inside. Finish the edge with a needle file.

RUB-OVER SETTING FOR OVAL STONES

To find the length of the bezel, add together the length and width of the stone, divide by 2 and multiply by π ($\pi = \frac{22}{7}$ or 3.141).

For example:

$$(\tfrac{3}{16} \text{ inch} + \tfrac{1}{4} \text{ inch}) \div 2 \times \pi = 21.98$$
$$= \tfrac{15}{16} \text{ inch}$$

Add the length of the bezel to $1\frac{1}{2}$ times the thickness of the silver. If you are using 22-gauge silver, the calculation will be: $\frac{15}{16} + \frac{1}{8}$ inch $= 1\frac{1}{16}$ inches.

1 Cut out a strip of silver $1\frac{1}{16}$ inches long; and the width necessary for your stone. Anneal the metal, bring the two ends together and solder. File off any excess solder from inside the bezel and tap it into shape on a mandrel.

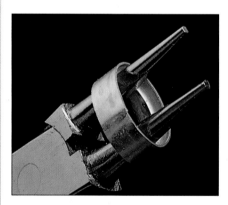

2 Using your round-nose pliers and with the joint of the bezel at the side, slip the bezel over the pliers and pull it to form an oval. If you have an oval mandrel, put the bezel onto the mandrel and tap it into shape with a rawhide mallet.

3 Check that the bezel fits the stone and adjust it as for the round bezel. Proceed as for the round bezel.

SETTING THE STONE

After all the work is completed on the piece and it has been polished up to the "Hyfin" stage, you are ready to set the stone.

1 Hold a ring in a ring vise and set a brooch or neckpiece into setter's wax or pitch. Leave the wax or pitch to harden, because the work must be really steady.

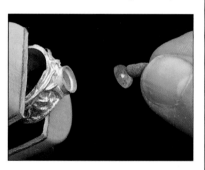

2 File the top edge of the bezel so that it is smooth and flat, and clean off any file marks with wet and dry paper. Use either a stone holder or a piece of modeling clay to hold the stone and place it in the setting.

3 Using a straight or curved highly polished burnisher, press over the edge of the setting at 12 o'clock, move down to 6 o'clock, across to 9 o'clock followed by 3 o'clock. Continue pressing with a smooth motion all the way around until the whole circumference is pressed down onto the stone. The bezel rocker is used in a similar way except that a rocking motion is used.

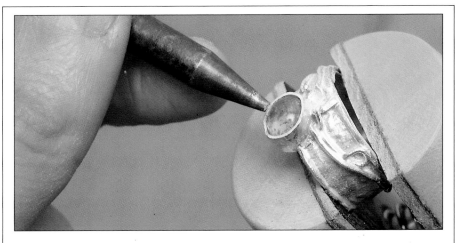

Simple rub-over settings. Daphne Krinos.

4 On heavier settings it is necessary to use a small punch with a hammer. Work in the same order as with a burnisher, gently tapping the punch at an angle of about 45° until all the bezel is resting on the stone. Take care not to mark the silver outside the bezel with the corner of the punch because deep marks are difficult to remove.

If the top surface of the setting has become uneven, either work gently around with the engraver to flatten it, and leave a shiny surface, or file around it, taking care not to mark the stone. After setting with a punch, a fine needle file will remove the marks of the punch, and the setting can then be polished with a suede stick.

SETTING UNCUT AND IRREGULAR-SHAPED STONES

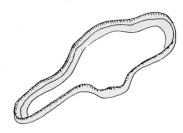

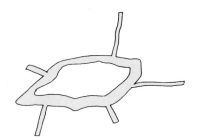

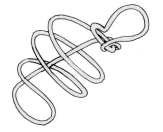

A simple rub-over setting can be made for a smooth stone by making a bezel to fit the shape of the stone, soldering the bezel to a base, and cutting away as much of the base as possible, leaving just enough for the stone to be supported.

A setting for a stone with an irregular surface can be made by cutting out a shape from fairly thin silver in which the bottom of the stone can sit and including different length prongs to hold the stone in place.

A conical stone can be set by wrapping wires either snugly or loosely around the stone. Start at the top and leave an end length turned into a loop. Wrap the other end around the stone as you want, and bring it back up to the top where it can be wrapped around the loop to tighten it. Cut off the wire and file the ends smooth.

Uncut stones

pink tourmaline crystal   **ruby crystal**   **blue topaz crystal**   **fluorspar crystal**   **tanzanite crystal**   **amber rough**

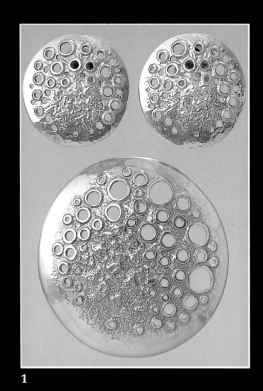

1

3

2

1 Reticulated earrings
and brooch with
pierced holes. Alan
Vallis.

2 Reticulated earrings.
Alan Vallis.

3 Symbol necklace and
earrings with
planished surface.
Alan Vallis.

1

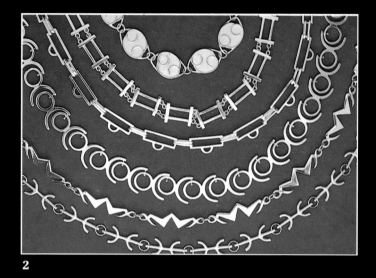

2

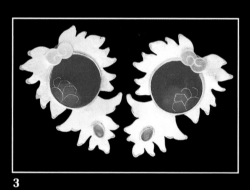

3

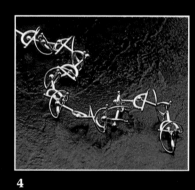

4

5

1 Textured necklace with
   carnelian. Alan Vallis.

2 Silver chains. Jinks
   McGrath.

3 Textured silver earrings
   with gold tips set with
   enameled domes and
   moonstones. Jinks
   McGrath.

4 This necklace shows the
   intricate use of wire. Brett
   Payne.

5 Oxidised silver and
   gold earrings with
   acrylic centres. Daphne
   Krinos.

PROJECT Silver Ring Set with Oval Lapis Lazuli

TO MAKE THE RING

YOU WILL NEED

Ring mandrel
Mandrel
Binding wire
Wire cutters
Ruler
Silver sheet 3¼ × ¾ inch (16 gauge)
Ring template
Files
Flux and solder
Bearer wire (1½ × ¼ inch)
Lapis lazuli (½ × ⅖ inch)
Polish
Ring clamp or vise
Burnisher or punch and hammer
Wet and dry papers

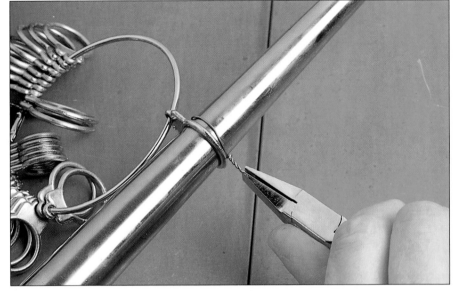

2

1 Measure the finger with ring sizers; I have made size 0.

2 Slide your ring sizer over the mandrel. Cut a length of binding wire, wrap it around the mandrel next to the ring sizer, and twist it firmly.

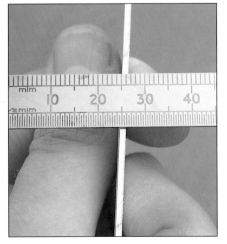

3

3 Take the wire off the mandrel, make a cut in it, and straighten it out.

4 Measure the length of the wire against your ruler.

5 Add to the length of the wire 1½ times the thickness of the silver you are going to use for the ring.

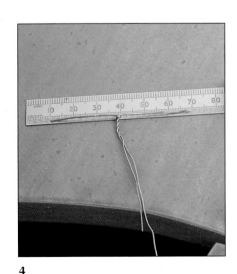

4

5

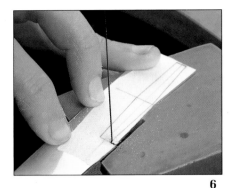

6

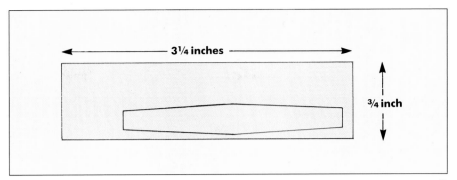

3¼ inches

¾ inch

8

6 Trace the pattern for the ring shank using the template, adjust the length to fit, and transfer the design to the silver. Pierce it out.

7 File off the square edges on both the inside and outside with a flat and oval file, and leave the ends flat.

8 Anneal, quench, rinse, and dry the silver.

9 Bend up the ends of the silver and fit them closely together, although it is not necessary for the ring to be round at this stage.

7

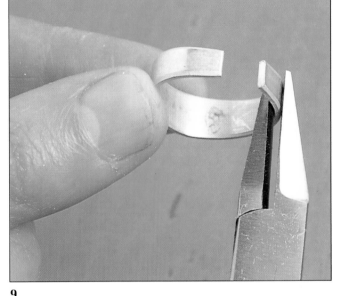

9

10

10 Flux the joint and solder with hard solder. Quench, rinse, and dry.

11 File off any excess solder from the inside of the ring. Make the ring round on the mandrel and file off excess solder from the outside.

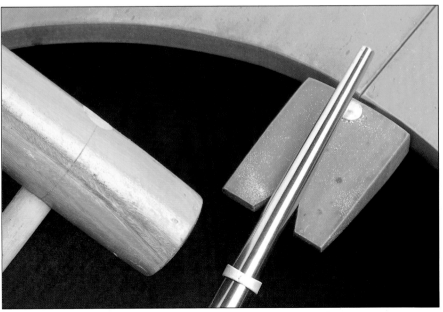

11

TO MAKE THE SETTING

The bezel must be made to fit both the stone and the curve of the ring. I therefore used bearer wire for the setting. For convenience metric figures are used in the formula.

1 Calculate the length of the bezel.

$$(14 + 10) \div 2 \times \pi = 37.7\text{mm}$$

Add 1½ times the thickness of the base edge of the bearer wire

$$1.5 + 37.7 = \text{approx. } 39.5\text{mm}$$

2 Cut off the required length of wire. Anneal, quench, rinse, and dry.

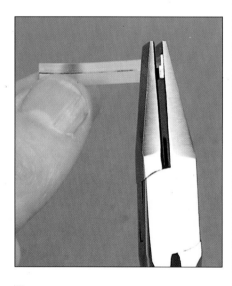

3 Bend up the ends to fit, flux the joint, and solder using hard solder. Quench, rinse, and dry.

4 Make the setting oval. Check that the stone fits and make any necessary adjustments.

TO MAKE THE SETTING FIT THE RING

1 Use an oval file to file the base of the setting to fit the curve of the ring until it sits snugly on top.

2 Make sure the ring and setting are clean, flux the bottom of the setting, and secure it to the ring with binding wire.

3 Solder the two together with easy solder. Pickle and rinse. Clean the ring with pumice paste.

4 File away any excess solder with a needle file, then work down through grades of wet and dry (used dry) papers.

5 Polish the ring, first with Tripoli, then with Hyfin. Polish the inside of the ring by hand or on a ring cone. Hold the ring in both hands while you polish it.

TO SET THE STONE

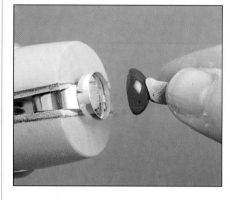

1 Hold the shank of the ring in a ring clamp or in the safe jaws of your vise. Place the stone in the setting.

2 Use your burnisher to push down on the two longer ends and then at the two sides. Continue rubbing all around the setting until it rests snugly over the stone. If you find that the silver is too hard to push over with a burnisher, use a punch and hammer in the same sequence.

3 Clean the setting and then polish the whole ring with jeweler's rouge, taking care not to get polish on the stone.

PROJECT Set of Earrings and Brooch

YOU WILL NEED

Silver sheet (24 gauge × 1¼ × 1⅜ inches) for domes; 18 gauge × 2 × 2½ inches and 24 gauge × 3⅛ × ⅜ inch for settings)

Texturing equipment

Scribe

Files

Moonstones (one ¾ inch across and two ½ inch across)

Templates

Drill

Mandrel

Flux and solder

Charcoal block

Polish

Fichu joint or silver fitting ⅜ × ¹⁄₁₀ inch (for brooch)

Safety catch or 18-gauge round silver wire (for brooch)

20-gauge silver wire (for ear stud and for ear loop)

Vise

Insulated tweezers

Jeweler's wax or pitch

Punches and hammer

Doming block

TO MAKE TEXTURED DOMES

1 Take a piece of 24 gauge silver sheet 1¼ × 1⅜ inches and texture the surface. The silver here was planished over a doming block. On the reverse side of the silver mark three circles, one with a diameter of ¾ inch and two with diameters of ½ inch. To make the piercing easier, scribe a slightly larger circle around the outside of each one and pierce between the lines. File to the inner line. Anneal, quench, rinse, and dry.

2 Place the ¾-inch diameter circle, textured side down, on your doming block. The dome should be slightly larger than the circle. Use a wooden or metal punch the same size as the dome, and punch the metal down. Repeat the process with smaller domes until the circle measures approximately ¹¹⁄₁₆ inch across. Do the same with the two ½-inch diameter circles until they measure approximately ⁷⁄₁₆ inch across.

1¼ inches

1⁵⁄₁₆ inches

TO MAKE SETTINGS FOR STONES

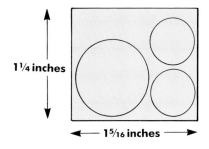

The bezel lengths are cut for the settings.

1 Use the 24-gauge silver sheet measuring 3⅛ × ⅜ inch to cut out three strips for the settings. These should be approximately 1½ inches long for the ½-inch stones and 2¼ inches long for the ¾-inch stones.

2 To determine the width of the settings, measure one-third of the height of the stones. These will make open settings when soldered to the surrounds.

TO MAKE THE SURROUNDS

1 Take the 18-gauge silver sheet measuring 2 × 2½ inches and transfer the pattern of the earrings and brooch to it. Drill holes in the center of each star and pierce out.

2 Pierce out the shape of the surrounds, leaving the bottom edges straight for the time being.

3 If you are using textured domes, place these on the pierced-out pattern, scribe closely around the outside of the dome, then scribe another line approximately ¹/₁₆ inch inside the first line. Pierce out that circle, file, and clean the edges.

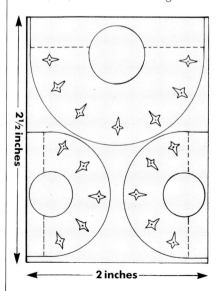

SOLDERING

1 Use hard solder to solder the bezels for the stones and make them round on your mandrel.

2 Place the bezels in the correct position on the surrounds, add flux, and place paillons of hard solder around the outside of the joints. Solder, quench, rinse, and dry.

3 Make open settings for the stones by piercing away the backs of the settings. Remember to leave enough silver for the stones to sit on.

4 Place the textured domes in position, flux, place small paillons of hard solder around the joints, and solder.

5 Working on the larger surround first, heat the surround, then bring the flame onto the setting or dome so that the solder runs. Repeat for the other two surrounds. Pickle, rinse, and dry before cleaning with pumice powder. Now pierce along the straight bottom edge and close around the domes or bezels. File the edges neatly.

MAKING THE BROOCH FITTINGS

1 You can either buy a fichu joint or make one from 18-gauge silver ¹/₁₀ × ³/₈ inch. Use a triangular needle file to make two straight lines up the silver, ¹/₁₀ inch from each end. Bend up the corners with flat-nose pliers and run hard solder into them. Drill a hole about ¹/₃₂ inch wide in the center of each side and file a notch in the center of the middle section.

2 Either buy a safety catch or make one from 18-gauge round wire, filed down at one end to a point. Use half-round or round-nose pliers to bend the wire into a loop. Bring the other end around to sit on the silver. File the bottom edge of the wire flat to guarantee good contact.

FINDINGS FOR THE EARRINGS

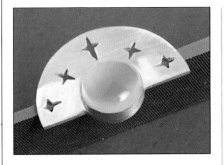 

1 Find the balancing point by placing the earring (and stone or textured dome) on the edge of a metal ruler or file. Mark the position.

2 To make an ear stud, cut a piece of 20-gauge silver wire and file straight across one end. Add flux and run a piece of easy solder onto it. Place some flux and a paillon of easy solder on the position you marked on the earring and position the earring on the soldering block, heating it through until the solder begins to run. Hold the wire pin with insulated tweezers and bring it down onto the work. Watch the solder flow while you hold it in position. Pickle, rinse, and clean with pumice powder. File the wire to a point, clean with papers, and burnish.

3 Make a loop using 20-gauge silver wire and form it into a jump ring with hard solder. Flatten the soldered side by holding about three-quarters of the ring in the safe jaws of a vise or in parallel pliers and tapping the protruding section with a hammer until it is flat. Put flux and a paillon of easy solder on the point you marked on the earring (place it above or below a star if necessary), place the earring on the soldering block, and heat through until the easy solder starts to run. Hold the ring in the insulated tweezers, bring it down on the work, and hold it in position while you watch the solder flow. Pickle, rinse, and clean with pumice powder. Fix an ear wire to the loop after polishing and setting the stone.

CLEANING AND POLISHING

After pickling and rinsing the brooch and earrings, clean them carefully with pumice paste. File away all excess solder, covering any textured areas with masking tape if necessary. Work through the grades of wet and dry (used dry) papers to remove any scratches. Hold the pieces in both hands to polish them, first with Tripoli polish. Remove any traces of polish with detergent before using Hyfin. Set the stones and finally polish with jeweler's rouge.

SOLDERING THE BROOCH FITTINGS

1 Place the fichu joint in position on the silver, making sure that the brooch will sit correctly. Flux the joint and place paillons of easy solder at each corner. Flux the underside of the safety catch – if you are using a ready-made catch, make sure that no flux runs up the inside – and run a paillon of easy solder onto it.

2 Place some flux and a paillon of easy solder where you want the safety catch to be. It should be at a slight angle to the fichu joint to give a firmer hold for the pin. Hold the safety catch in a pair of insulated tweezers and flux the bottom again.

3 Support the work in a charcoal block and heat it slowly, making sure that the large area of silver is heated before you bring the flame onto the fichu joint for the solder to run. As the solder for the safety catch runs, lower it onto the work and hold it steady. Remove the flame, still holding it steady, then pickle. Rinse, dry, and clean with pumice powder.

SETTING THE STONES

1 Before you set the stones, make sure the work is held securely in pitch or in jeweler's wax. Gently heat the pitch or wax and place your work in it. Allow the pitch or wax to cool slightly, then gently work it up around the edges of the piece.

2 Set the stones using either a punch and hammer or a burnisher.

3 Play a gentle flame around the edge of your work to soften the pitch or wax, and carefully prize up the piece with tweezers. Avoid playing the flame directly onto the stone. Remove excess pitch with turpentine and excess wax with acetone.

2

ATTACHING THE BROOCH PIN

Make the tag of the pin to fit the inside of the fichu joint, and rivet the pin in place.

OXIDIZING THE TEXTURED DOME

If you want to oxidize the textured dome, protect all the other parts of the work with beeswax or stop-out varnish. Immerse all the pieces in a hot solution of potassium sulfide for about a minute, suspending them on fine silver wire attached to the fittings.

If oxidization occurs on areas that you had hoped to keep shiny, heat the whole piece up gently and quench in acid, which will eliminate the problem. However, you will have to start again with the potassium sulfide. Small areas of oxidization may be removed by careful polishing – preferably by hand – and you can bring highlights to the domes by gently rubbing them with the burnisher.

The finished pieces

Technical Information

ANNEALING TEMPERATURES

	°F	°C
Copper	700–1200	370–650
Brass	800–1380	430–750
Gold (not 24 carat)	1200–1380	650–750
Silver	1120–1300	600–700

MELTING TEMPERATURES

	°F	°C
Copper	1980	1080
Brass	1660	900
Gold (not 24 carat)	1600–1830	880–1000
Silver	1640	890

SOLDER MELTING TEMPERATURES

| | Hard | | Medium | | Easy | |
	°F	°C	°F	°C	°F	°C
9 carat Gold	1390–1465	755–795	1355–1390	735–755	1330–1200	720–650
14 carat Gold	1380–1445	750–785	—	—	1310–1350	710–730
18 carat Gold	1455–1525	790–830	1350–1410	730–765	1290–1320	700–715
Silver	1375–1430	745–778	1330–1410	720–765	1300–1340	705–725

SPECIFIC GRAVITIES

	%	oz/in³	gm/mm³
Platinum	21.5	11.74	20.34
Copper	8.93		
Gold	19.36	10.00	17.33
Fine Silver	10.56	5.74	9.95
Sterling Silver	10.40	5.68	9.84
18 carat Gold	16.13	9.32	16.15
9 carat Gold	12.27	7.09	12.29
14 carat Gold	14.83	8.57	14.85
Water	1.00	0.58	1.00
Plastic	1.20	0.70	1.21

TO CALCULATE WEIGHT OF SILVER AND GOLD SHEET

Sheet 50 × 100 × 1mm:

Weight = volume × density. For example, to find the weight of a:

Silver sheet:
$2 \times 4 \times 0.39in \times 5.68 = 1.772oz$
$50 \times 100 \times 1mm \times 9.84 = 49.2gm$

Gold sheet (18 karat):
$2 \times 4 \times 0.39in \times 9.32 = 2.907oz$
$50 \times 100 \times 1mm \times 16.15 = 80.7gm$

To estimate the cost of the silver or gold in a piece of jewelry, you must first know, or estimate, the weight. Multiply the weight by the cost per gram or oz of the metal.

DIMENSIONS OF A CIRCLE

If your circle has a diameter of 10cm, the circumference can be calculated as follows:

	2πr[radius]	π × diameter
Fractions	$2 \times \frac{22}{7} \times 5 = 31.42$	$\frac{22}{7} \times 10 = 31.42$
Decimals	$2 \times 3.141 \times 5 = 31.41$	$3.141 \times 10 = 31.41$

The diameter of a circle is found by multiplying the known circumference by 0.31831.
The area of a circle is: diameter × itself × 0.7854.
For example, the area of a circle with a diameter of 14mm = $14 \times 14 \times 0.7854 = 153.93$ sq mm

The volume of a rod is: diameter × itself × 0.7854 × height. For example,
the volume of a rod with a diameter of 3cm and 10cm high = $3 \times 3 \times 0.7854 \times 10 = 70.68$ cu cm

BROWNE & SHARPS METAL GAUGE (or thickness)

Gauge	inch	mm
7	0.020	0.5
8	0.022	0.55
9	0.024	0.6
10	0.028	0.7
11	0.032	0.8
12	0.035	0.9
13	0.037	0.95
14	0.043	1.1
15	0.047	1.2
16	0.051	1.3
18	0.059	1.5
20	0.065	1.65
22	0.073	1.85
24	0.083	2.1
28	0.126	3.2

WEIGHTS

Troy ounces are used in weighing precious metals:
1 troy ounce = 31.104gm

Avoirdupois ounces are used in weighing base metals:
1 avoirdupois ounce = 28.35gm

CARAT WEIGHT USED FOR WEIGHING STONES

1 carat = ⅕ gram

Carats are divided into points:
1 carat = 100 points
½ carat = 0.50 points
¼ carat = 0.25 points